AF481132

Kiko's Journal

Written by: Harry Brodsky
Illustrated by: Dani Thompson

My name is Kiko. I love to explore.
I've seen my whole town, I'd love to see more.

Should I take a trip? Yeah that's what I'll do.
I'll go and explore, I'll see some place new.

But where should I go? And what should it be?
What kind of new place do I want to see?

Maybe a city?

Or maybe a fair?

Maybe the ocean?
I haven't been there.

Oh yes I am sure, I've made up my mind.
I'll go to the moon and see what I find.

What an adventure, I really can't wait.
Exploring the moon is sure to be great.

Except for one thing, I'm sorry to say.
The moon and its sights are so far away.

This is a problem, a problem indeed.
Finding its answer is just what I need.

I know what I'll do! I'll stack and I'll stack.
I'll build up some steps
with wood that's out back.

I'm so excited to go to the moon.
Time to get building, I'll write again soon.

Joe's HARDWARE
Luna's MARKET
It took a whole day. The building was fun.
I'm writing this time from step number one.

Up here I can see a little bit more.
The roof of my house, the grocery store.

Tomorrow will be more stacking and views,
but now it is night and time for a snooze.

More and more building all day in the sun.
Now step number two is finally done.

Still far from the moon, but when I look down,
I'm high up enough to see my whole town.

The pines in the park, the shops and the school.
But now I must rest, it's time to refuel.

I think I can say from what I can see,
that work is complete on step number three.

Out in the distance the big city sits.
The skyscrapers stand wherever one fits.

Truly amazing, a beautiful sight.
I feel inspired, for now though, goodnight.

Hello once again. I'm tired and sore.
It's getting high up on step number four.

Way far down below, the birds do their dance.
And even the cars are looking like ants.

There's stars in the sky, it's hard not to stare.
I'll write more tomorrow with way more to share.

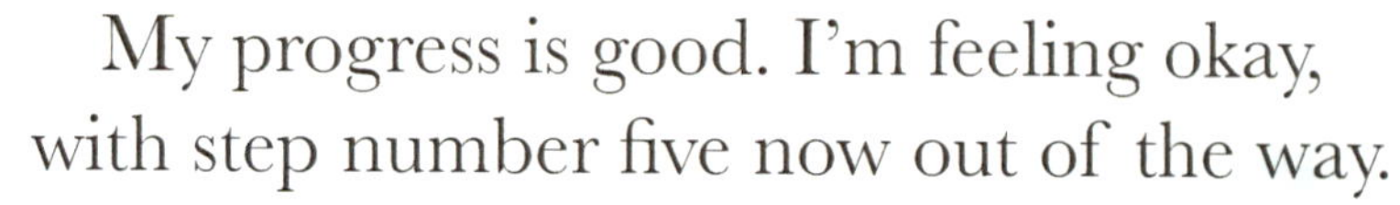

My progress is good. I'm feeling okay,
with step number five now out of the way.

The big city cars and big city crowds.
Tucked deep underneath the big puffy clouds.

Miles and miles of marshmallow sky.
It's making me sleepy, it's no wonder why.

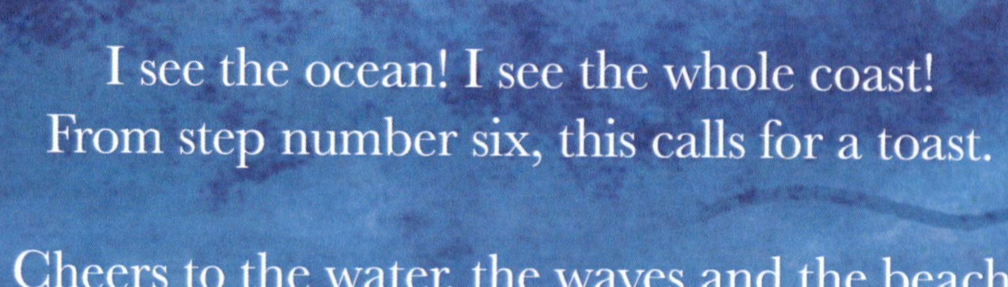

I see the ocean! I see the whole coast!
From step number six, this calls for a toast.

Cheers to the water, the waves and the beach.
And cheers to the moon, still out of my reach.

The trip of all trips. The ultimate prize.
The ocean and moon. A sight for sore eyes.

Step number seven seems sturdy and strong.
I feel no wobbles. I hope I'm not wrong.

I see my country and all of its parts.
I see where it ends, I see where it starts.

The cities and towns, the farms and the green.
It's time to enjoy this marvelous scene.

I want to check in before it gets late.
I'm here to say hi from step number eight.

Above the whole world, all water and land.
A big ball of life, so kooky and grand.

It turns and it spins. There's so much to roam.
This big ball of life, I'm proud it's my home.

I'm in outer space!
I see the moon shine.
I can spot craters
from step number nine.

The world looks so small, a green and blue blip.
Too far to tumble, I hope I don't slip.

With every new step, I feel a new ache.
It takes so much work, my bones need a break.

I've got some good news.
This build was a blast
and step number ten
is finished at last!

Closer than ever, I'm just about there.
The moon sits and waits, I can't help but stare.

For now I will watch this view I adore.
Tomorrow will be my time to explore.

KIKO
WAS HERE

Today was the day! I walked on the moon!
I took my first steps not long after noon.

I had a great time. I knew that I would.
I did so much stuff. As much as I could.

I dug through the dirt.

I picked up some rocks.

I slid inside craters.

There's dust in my socks!

I ran extra fast and jumped extra high.

My body felt light. I thought I could fly.

I searched the whole moon,
each crack and each fold.
Even the dark side, wow it was cold!

I saw a rover. It drove very slow.
And also a flag, no aliens though.

I walked on the moon, that's hard to achieve.
But now it is time to pack up and leave.

When I first started, my goal was so far.
A trip to the moon with no plane or car.

Then bit by bit, I made the whole climb.
And I reached my goal, one step at a time.

KIKO WAS HERE